I had a moment.

Jordan Granger

BookLeaf Publishing

Presentation by *BookLeaf Publishing*

Web: www.bookleafpub.com

E-mail: info@bookleafpub.com

ISBN: 9789357213059

First edition 2023

Self portrait.

She is petite,
five feet tall.
Hair an unnatural shade of blonde,
brunette banished by bleach.
A peroxide 'Barbie'.
Tired hazel eyes streaked with amber,
tiny specks of gold.
Delicately irregular nose,
Imperfect but perfectly passed on.
Two dainty lips tinted rose,
from where sweet voice escapes.
Upon dimpled cheek lay fine freckle,
small kisses from the sun.
Skin uncreased,
patient and soft.
Until the fire burns her soul,
causing change of face.
The calm before the storm.
Saddened soul wept,
silent tears, forbidden freedom.
But she'll forgive, it's who she is,
a master in disguise.

My pack.

Just a puppy when we met,
love strong from the start.
She kissed my nose,
and placed me into her heart.
She took me to her home,
introduced me to her pack.
She taught me fun tricks;
Spin, Speak, Sing, for snacks.
She lets me sleep in her bed,
every single night.
I stay close to my human,
until the dark becomes light.
And when we wake up,
I lick her sleepy face.
Good morning routine,
stretch, lick, warm embrace.
She waits while I enjoy the smells,
On our walks long and muddy.
I bark at other dogs,
It's pups duty to protect best buddy.
I am her family,
And she is my pack.
Ill love her forever,

Gimme a snack?

To my parents.

Cheri.
The most beautiful of mothers,
my sweet guardian angel.
Bearer of darling sisters,
epitome of joy.
Most nurturing,
compassionate and beloved.
Forever treasuring our time,
gossiping and laughing together.
Our bike rides, muddy
left stains on my heart.
Many a fond memory,
shared with my mother.
I'll love her,
Forever.

Stephen.
The most loving of fathers,
my loyal protector.
Moved Heaven and Earth,
just for me.
Tough but adoring,
devoted to six.
Forever treasuring our time,
playing card games and late night tv bingeing.

Making jokes together,
the best of buds.
Many a fond memory,
shared with my father.
I'll love him,
Forever.

To my sisters.

Abigail,
As much as I annoy you,
and wind you up.
You know I love you,
very dearly.
You're sister and best bro,
all in one.
Our brains connected,
telepathic.
You always know what I'm thinking,
Before I've even thought it.
Thanks for not snitching,
'Jellyfish fields'.
I love you.

Imogen,
I remember the day,
that you were born.
Invoked my motherly instincts.
I was very protective,
over tiny baby you.
Now eleven years on,
I feel the same.
I still see you as,
tiny tumbling toddler.

But you've grown up so fast,
into beautiful young woman.
My best buddy and 'pea pod'.
I'll treasure you forever,
eternally proud of who you are.
Never change,
I love you.

Eilidh,
It seems like just yesterday,
our parents brought you home.
Beautiful beloved baby.
Ten years later,
you're my height.
Stealing my clothes,
like you stole my heart.
You're away with the fairies,
head in the clouds.
'Little space cadet'.
Never change who you are,
don't let the bullies win.
You are perfect,
just the way you are.
I love you.

Mina,
Little Mina-Scarlett,
the smallest of us all.
Don't grow up too fast,

stay innocent and sweet.
Enjoy being a child,
stay compassionate but carefree.
My tiny doppelgänger,
the other half of my soul.
Such a big heart,
inside such tiny person.
You never cease to amaze me.
Beautiful baby ‘bean’,
I love you.

Small fish

Dreaming of the sea
The small fish with golden scales
Wishing to be free

You are there

You are there,
during my darkest days
guiding me to light.

You are there,
when my heart is broken
picking up my pieces.

You are there,
when my eyes weep sorrow
wiping the tears away.

You are there,
the centre of many happy memories
laughing by my side.

You are there,
a great romance of my young life,
My best friend.

- Emmie-Jayne, I love you.

For Dan, the mushroom man

Sunshine hides behind grey curtain
of thick, fierce cloud.
Traipsing through maze of forest green
twigs snap under steady foot.
Birdsong comes loud and sweet
a private treetop symphony.
My friend, the man with mousey hair
experienced mushroom hunter.
There's talk of everything and nothing
our voices echo on.
Almost missing natures gift.
The blusher mushroom, sliced turns pink.
Bay boletes with brick colour cap.
The fungi gowned in lilac dress
Amethyst deceiver.
Then there's folklores favourite, fly agaric.
Crimson red with small white spots.
Home of the intoxicated fairies.
Stray windswept pinecone
coming back with me.
As we leave the forest in our shadows
at days end, homeward bound.
A walk with my friend
is a day well spent.

Sunday morning.

S- Slept late into the morning,
U- underneath duck down embrace.
N- Net curtains flowing, by window left open.
D- Day of rest.
A- Admiring still slumbering dog, dreaming.
Y- Yellow sunlight dances on the ceiling.

M- Mischievous sisters giggling,
O- outside my bedroom door.
R- 'Rise and shine' in singsong voices.
N- Noon fast approaching, bed I must leave.
I - In the kitchen, mother makes breakfast.
N- Newly brewed pot of tea, waiting for me.
G- Glorious Sunday, my favourite day.

Skiing in Megeve.

The world still sleeping,
on bright winters dawn.
After a snow filled twilight,
resting on cold creaking bench.
High upon snowy Rochebrune.
Breath-taking views,
a panorama of beauty.
Megeves marvellous mountains.
Gazing from impressive height,
unforgettable resort in white.
Early air bitterly cold,
leaving face flushed pink.
The slopes fresh and powdery,
untracked and full of promise.
Adjusting my goggles.
Before tipping skis,
over dauntingly steep edge.
Heart pounding,
adrenaline shooting through my veins.
Soaring down sun kissed slope,
My mind finally silent…

The base of the mountain,
my only thought.

Eunice.

Mother Natures mad,

storm Eunice is raging on.

Listen for her wail.

Trust

Hope
Sweet, All powerful
Wish, dream, pray
Ever so illusive
Trust.

The circus.

Across big tops threshold,
waits a whole new world.
A unique existence,
a passionate life.
Eager crowds fill every seat,
anticipation escalating.
A single spotlight shines,
upon blue haired clown.
Followed by a kaleidoscope of colour,
applause uproars.
Louder than lions banned from act.
Knives thrown by beautiful woman,
concentration unwavering.
Fearless man,
walking above anxious crowd.
On rope so thin,
it could be invisible.
The greatest act.
She climbs high,
twists and twirls.
Wrapped around flowing fabric,
floating in the air.
From the edge of my seat,
heart residing in mouth.
Aerial acrobat falls.

plummeting down,
into unacknowledged waters.
Overwhelming relief,
spreads like wildfires.
While blue haired clown manic,
cackles at our terror.

Paralymic Pride.

- Tokyo Paralympics 2020/21
  Wheelchair Rugby.

They sit stoically,
awaiting the signal.
Like lions pride.
They stalk their prey,
with fierce locked eyes.
Ready to strike,
GB VS US.

A momentary silence,
as whistle blows.
Adrenaline sparked,
And teamwork surges.
Once quiet sports hall,
now electric.
The sounds of ‘murder ball’
raging on.
Ferocious titanium crashes,
brutality brings bruises.
Screams of support and tactic,
from strong female player
injured courtside.
Driven by determination,

Unshaken by discrimination.
The pride charges on.
Through Blood Sweat and Tears.
Triumph and domination,
overwhelming emotions.
An energy indescribable.
Prides rejoice,
in great golden victory.
As Team GB make history.

#impossibletoignore

We stand with Ukraine.

Shells and bombs,
rained down on Ukraine.
Their once bustling streets,
now sparse and bleak.
Russia has initiated invasion,
such selfish purpose.
Shattering peace in Europe,
the destruction colossal.
Innocent hospital struck,
In heinous air strike.
Slaughter of the innocent,
frightened families flee.
Children ripped from parents' arms;
Their next embrace,
Uncertain.
Prams left at polish stations,
for refugee mothers inbound.
Hearts broken and tears shed,
Letters written 'just in case'.
All genders fight together,
Bearing arms.
Side by side,
no time for discrimination,
with threats of consequences.
'To the likes of which, you have never seen.'

But..
In these dark times,
There is support far and wide.
We stand with Ukraine.

Swimming.

Light against the water.

Tiny bubbles dancing around me,

floating in silence.

Castle Varrich (Caisteal Bharraich)

- Castle Varrich, Tongue, Scottish Highlands.

On sombre mind,
my thoughts do wander.
They make their way back,
to my favourite place.

Across the river,
where white water waits.
Guided by rickety bridge
leading to natures gate.

Pass the threshold,
listen to the song of the wind.
See the trees dressed in green gowns,
dancing together as one.

Amble upland,
on rugged spiral path.
The scent in the air abandoned by rain
petrichor.

Upon the summit,
solitary castle with mismatched walls.

A panorama of breath-taking views.
Taken aback, my dear Scotland.
Caisteal Bharraich.
My favourite place.

You.

Darling you'd linger

even if I lost my mind

I'll remember you

Untitled.

Underneath incandescent moon,
the stars looked down with jealousy.
On solitary winding track,
two loving souls becoming one.
Trembling voices echo in the silence.
Cold delicate fingers wandering,
tracing the silhouettes
on nude pale thigh.
Heavy breath dancing,
between deep passionate kisses exchanged.
In bitterly cold air, sharing their warmth.
With bare begging bodies,
intertwined upon cold blue bonnet.
Rough loving hand around her throat,
The other lingering upon exposed breast.
Sweet longing whispers in ear.
Euphoric moans shatter the silence.
In unison glowing bodies,
quiver and quake.
During symphony's finale.
Underneath incandescent moon.
Two loving souls becoming one.

For the last time.

I watched you sleep soundly,
for the last time.
Traced your warm pale skin,
delicately with my fingers.
I kissed your forehead,
gently with my lips.
And I looked at you.
So at peace,
whilst my own thoughts, at war.
And the sadness lingered,
until moon was replaced by sun.

Now, The twenty sixth.
Scottish September skies,
kilted in grey cloud.
The cup of tea from the night before,
the packed up boxes,
on our bedroom floor.
And the way you looked at me,
for the last time.
A deafening silence,
no goodbye.

Depression.

D- Dreading waking up.
E- Even on the good days.
P- Preying on my thoughts.
R- Ruining the happy moments.
E- Everything seems worthless.
S- Siphoning my soul.
S- Still I stand.
I- Ignoring my demons.
O- Overcoming the darkness.
N- Never giving in.

The Reaper

Broken woman filled with dread,
sinking low into the bathtub.
Slashed deep, clear water tainted red.
Now before her The Reaper stands,
fleshless boney hand, reaching out.
He whispers the promise of heavenly land.

Torn dragging cloak, dark as coal.
Looming hood masking faceless man,
he whispers the promise of cherished soul.
He heard her sorrow from afar,
Benevolent, his comfort he will give her.
He whispers the promise of unseen scars.

Her body motionless now heavy as lead,
tiny last air bubbles, pale and cold.
Her soul travels to the land of the dead.
The Reaper guides her onto humble boat,
grasping her hand in his own.
To heaven they will float

www.ingramcontent.com/pod-product-compliance
Lightning Source LLC
Chambersburg PA
CBHW051757130826
49812CB00033B/1184
9789357213059